Alberto
GIACOMETTI

<u>I certainly practise painting…</u>

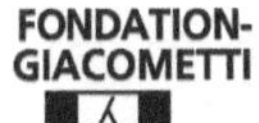

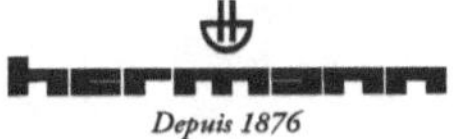

Je fais certainement la peinture
et la sculpture. Et cela depuis
toujours, depuis la première
fois que j'ai dessiné ou
peint, pour mordre sur
la réalité, pour me
défendre, pour me nourrir
pour grossir, grossir
pour mieux me défendre
pour gagner le plus
possible sur tous les
plans et dans tous les
domaines dans toutes les directions pour me défendre
contre la famine, contre
le froid contre la mort
pour être le plus libre
possible, le plus libre

Preparatory manuscript for the text "I certainly practise
painting", June 1957
Blue ink on paper, 20.7 x 26.9 cm (unfolded paper)
Fondation Giacometti Archives

<u>1901</u>
Son of the painter Giovanni Giacometti, the best
representative of Impressionism in Switzerland (…).

<u>up to 1915</u>
Introduced to the arts through his father's work as well as
the books, albums and publications he found in his father's
office. Particularly interested in the great painters who were
at the same time brilliant draughtsmen, among them Dürer,
~~Rubens~~ and Rembrandt.

<u>1913</u>
Did his first painting, 'apples'.

Extract of 'Dates biographiques', preparatory typescript for the
autobiography published in Jacques Dupin's book,
Alberto Giacometti, Editions Maeght, 1962

If I had some advice to give to a young painter, I would tell him to start by copying an apple.

Rinascita, no. 8, 23 June 1962
(translated from the Italian)

Fragments of a diary
In conversation with Gotthard Jedlicka

<u>30 March 1953</u>

*When Alberto Giacometti talks about his father, which
is often, I realise to what degree he feels grateful to him.*
'**My father was very, very, very kind**', he says – all
the time emphasising the '**very**' as if he wanted to
put a full stop, though a temporary one. 'As soon as
we became adolescents, my father allowed us to be
free to do what we wanted. He gave us advice when
we asked for it, but once it had been given, he left
it at that. He didn't force me to go to Schiers, but
he thought I had to try finding my way there. At
the time, I was not sure what profession I wanted
to choose: sculptor, painter, or even chemist. At
Schiers, I was able to set up a little studio, equipped
with all the tools necessary to work as a sculptor
or a painter, and that's where I spent all my free
time. The teachers and the other students left me to
it. After having successfully passed the first part of
my examinations, I asked my father if I could have
a three months' sabbatical to think about my future.
I took myself very seriously in those days! My father
and my teachers accepted my choice as if it was the
most natural thing in the world. We had agreed on a
date for my return though: without taking the end of
the year exam. But once the three months' sabbatical
ended, I didn't feel like going back to Schiers. Was
it actually the right decision not to go back? I'm not
sure. My father didn't object and said that my mother
wouldn't object either for, all said and done, she had
married a painter. 'Do you want to be a painter?'
my father asked. 'A painter or a sculptor', I replied.

He advised me to try my luck at Geneva's School
of Fine Arts – advice I followed: I stayed there three
days. A little while later, I accompanied my father
to the Venice Biennale, and after that, he thought
it might be good for me to go to Paris to work in a
free Academy like he had done in his youth, at the
Grande Chaumière; to draw and to paint: which I
didn't want at first, but as my father didn't insist, I
decided to go. When he paid me a visit, on one of
the very first days, he accompanied me to the Grande
Chaumière, sat among the students, and started
drawing and painting: he felt, as he said, like staying
in Paris to start afresh. **'Yes, my father was very, very
kind.'** And after a pause: **'very!'**

1 April 1953

Alberto Giacometti on Matisse: 'In November last
year, I met Matisse several times. I was at Tériade's,
in his house at Cap Ferrat. Matisse came to see us
almost every afternoon. He was brought by car. Being
Tériade's friend, he offered to make a bay window in
one of the rooms of his house. Because he was his
friend? Yes, but also because he couldn't feel happy
in an environment in which he was not represented
by one or several of his art works. And he set to
work, displaying an incredible amount of energy!
Meanwhile, he explained that the room also had to
be decorated with mosaics so that the window would
be shown to advantage. He attacked that task with
as much passion. In spite of his illness, which would
have paralysed a lot of others, he only thought of his

work. He was endowed with a prodigious memory. He was continuously talking about his youth, particularly the conversations between him and his father, mimicking the dialogues; he imitated his father's voice when the latter spoke, so much so that the conversation between father and son taking place in front of us were incredibly vivacious. And that's also how he related the conversations between his mother and father–with such emotion that he suddenly started to cry. **"Well, that's it: I've become senile!"** he said in a humbled sober voice: he was surprised by his own emotion, slightly sickened by it.'

Amongst the drawings tidied away in large worn folders, covered in plaster dust, through which we leaf together, he more hastily than I, are numerous reproductions: pen and ink drawings and pencil drawings of various formats and on assorted papers, partly on letter-writing paper, but also European masterpieces, especially European painting. We are looking for the drawing of a Parisian urban landscape that could be reproduced in my 'Journal parisien' whose publication is planned for next autumn by Suhrkamp editions. But that sheet proved impossible to find, even though Alberto Giacometti is adamant that at least one of the drawings of that landscape should be in one of the folders. Several times though we come across various reproductions. I tell Giacometti how much I'm surprised and happy. Copying great masters is no longer fashionable with artists of his generation. Does he think he has to

apologise to me for enjoying to work in that fashion?
'It has nothing to do with me,' *he says,* 'wherever I am,
when I see something that makes a lasting impression
on me I feel the need to capture the image in time,
and that pushes me to copying it. Is a copy anything
but an attempt to extract the maximum from an
encounter with a work of art? I'm convinced that the
copy of a masterpiece is the best school there is for
any artist who decides to make art. At all times, great
artists have been aware of that: Michelangelo made
copies of Giotto and Masaccio, Rubens of Titian,
Ingres of Raphael, and later, Delacroix of Rubens
and Rembrandt, Manet of Delacroix and Matisse
of Chardin and so on.'
'In reality, there's nothing better than copying to
understand it has always been and will always be
about the same thing: art. And one discovers and
one learns art through art. Obviously I don't always
make copies of the whole piece; often, I capture the
part of the work that speaks to me the most. Look
at that landscape! Is it not the most magnificent
cubist landscape there is? Don't you think it contains
everything an abstract painting is likely to contain?
I made the copy of that landscape from a painting
by Jan Van Eyck – and it's only by copying it that
I realised how modern it is!'
*Later on, he also shows me other copies, some from Giotto,
others from his entourage, for example a self-portrait by
his father. These reproductions help me to realise that he
takes his inspiration from a rich tradition; they are the
proof of his curiosity and artistic intelligence.*

*
**

*A moment before Alberto Giacometti gets ready to draw
my portrait, the first difficulty presents itself. He does own
a pencil (and for the time being, he only has one), but it is
blunt, and he has no knife to sharpen it.*

— *You don't have a knife?*

— Yes, of course I do, I have several different
knives!, *he protests.* And I bought them all for this
reason! But since then, I've used them for my
sculptures, for plaster, for clay–which blunt them
quickly–so I can no longer use them to sharpen
my pencils.

*I quickly realise that it's impossible to give him any advice,
like to put a knife aside to be used solely to sharpen pencils
or even to buy a pencil sharpener. For the drawing of this
portrait, he uses particularly large sheets. A little while
after starting the first drawing, he says:*

— It's not working! I'm sitting too close to you.
I can't see anything at all!

*With a piercing gaze he measures the distance between
him and me. He is seated, I am seated and he's thinking
about how to increase the distance between us both. He is
so deep in his thought, so concentrated that the wrinkles
and fine lines on his face are enhanced. There are two
solutions: either I get up and he places me elsewhere, or
he gets up and chooses another place to sit. Whatever the
solution, both seem bothersome, and in the end,
he leaves it at that.*

— I wish to go as far as possible, though.

Without interrupting his drawing activity, he comments:

— It's strange! Because I know you; I even

remember the hat you were wearing thirty years ago;
I'm going to draw it one more time! When I see you
walking towards me in the street, even from afar, you
seem familiar because of your gait, your appearance,
your face; because of that I feel I can draw you from
memory, with no difficulty whatsoever. But now that
you're sitting in front of me, you seem strange, if not
downright disturbing!
*For a moment his hand wanders on the paper as if it
had nothing to do being there; he doesn't pay me the least
attention.*
      — I find it hard to imagine I could have known
you.
*He scrutinises me in such a way that I have the impression
he's trying to pull me out of myself, and with his nicotine-
stained teeth, slightly spaced, he bites the skin between his
lower lip and his chin with some violence.*
      — I regret having had the weakness to accept
making your portrait!
*He continues drawing, and rarely lifts the pencil from
the sheet.*
      — It's completely different when it's my brother
Diego! It's been some years since he started posing
for me, and whatever I want and as often as I want,
be it a bust, a portrait or a drawing; so I'm starting
to be able to handle his face! But what am I talking
about! Able to handle?! Even when it's him posing for
me, it doesn't happen any other way with him. When
I sculpt, paint or draw, I always have him in mind.
*While looking straight into my eyes, his hand, pencil
between fingers, continues gliding on the paper, without
his eyes following his hand; the pencil scratches at the paper.*

— Painting portraits is a terribly complicated thing!
(He forgets he's in the habit of finding each task, in the field of visual arts, terribly complicated.)
I agree, politely:
— *Yes.*
— It's complicated because anyone – and one can easily become 'anyone' – decides to paint or draw a portrait which is 'a good likeness'. My God! 'Likeness', what does that mean?
For the first time, he interrupts his work and scrutinises irritably the tip of his yellow pencil.
— Did you know the answer?
— *No.*
— So?
He pulls himself together and continues drawing. When he is in that mood, it seems that talking encourages him.
— One should draw or paint the model as we see him, simply as we see him. Simply? That's precisely where the difficulty resides! Draw him as we see him and not as we know him. And not as we know what he should look like or as others remember having seen him! It's only by forgetting what we don't see that we can reach the essential likeness. When the portrait is alive, it's inevitably a good likeness!
He keeps quiet now, but very quickly, his own silence makes him impatient and to interrupt it he says:
— **What?!**
I don't have the answer to his question and I focus my attention on not moving, remaining as still as possible. (Though he doesn't seem to attach the least importance to that.)

He has no other choice than to carry on with his thinking:

— Here you are, sitting here!

His pencil stroke becomes even more insistent; he seems to want to pierce the paper, as if the decisive form was hiding behind.

— With each pencil stroke you seem to become more and more alien!

He shows me, demonstrates.

— Look! Look! With each stroke, I make you further away from me. But this stroke, what has it to do with you? And that one? If it continues, I will no longer see you at all.

Shaking his head violently, he stops again.

— Now that I've started drawing your portrait, I feel sufficiently inspired to continue! What do you say? Now I feel like continuing to draw you, even more, precisely because it seems impossible to accomplish it. At this precise moment, I'd like to have you pose for me for months. You pose so well! We shouldn't let it go! I beg you not to leave me high and dry here with my first attempts! I'm asking you, please! Let's continue!

I'm not going to give a detailed account of everything that's happened in those two hours. But the following episode seems to me important enough. He does four drawings successively, then he throws them one after another on the couch placed near me. After having thrown the fourth drawing on the pile with the three others, he gets up, running his fingers through his tousled hair.

— I should never have started!, *he says.* One should never start something one is not sure one can finish!

He walks towards the couch and tries to put the drawings next to each other, which is not easy for the couch is covered with enormous piles of books and magazines.
I say:

— *It's impossible to complete those drawings in* any other way than by leaving them as they are. With a first sketch—and here, we're talking about the first sketches—you're incapable of rendering what you hope to accomplish with the last drawing—as you yourself claim, incidentally!
He replies by pulling a face. After having scrutinised each drawing in turn from left to right, he nods again and says:

— Not one of them is worth anything!
With his index whose nail is encrusted with plaster, he points forcibly to the first drawing, then to the second, the third and finally the fourth, gradually getting all worked up, with a harsher and harsher tone of voice:

— Failed! Failed! Failed! Failed!!

— *For you perhaps, but not for me. Those drawings* are alive, I say to him, for it's my deepest conviction.
He scrutinises them one more time, with more determination this time.

— In each there is a beginning.
Adding to that—as if he regretted what he has just said—with a tone even more peremptory now:

— But in each there is a different beginning—that's the reason why none will go further than the other!

— *Each one has its reason to be.*

— If only I could draw! I don't know how to draw!
After a few moments of silence:

— And that's precisely the reason why
I continue to draw!
*He turns towards me and looks straight into my eyes as if
seeing me for the first time.*
— When I look at your head, I see something
that inspires the sculptor in me! And that's a mistake!
My God! When I try my hardest to draw you, your
face shouldn't inspire the sculptor in me, but the
draughtsman – or the painter if you like, but in any
case, not the sculptor!
*He places the sheets in a pile and puts them aside, face
down.*
— Do you intent to come back this summer?
If you do, I'll paint your portrait. I feel more at ease
with the brush than the pencil! You'll see! I'm already
agonising over the difficulties I'll have to face in our
next session!

<u>3 April 1953</u>

Alberto Giacometti:
— Have you ever been to Rudier's, in Vésinet?
— *No.*
— You've missed something! In the vast park of
Rudier, the founder, are sculptures by Rodin, Maillol,
Despiau and Laurens; as well as some bronzes by other
sculptors. It's a magnificent museum of contemporary
sculpture. Among those bronzes, the most beautiful is
a torso by Despiau! When I saw it the first time from
quite far away, I said to myself: 'Oh, a Chinese bronze!'
After, coming closer, I realised it was a sculpture by
Despiau. It resembles a Chinese sculpture though.

One feels that in his work, Despiau is facing a whole
universe. He doesn't experience the female body
like something which, before him, has already been
represented many times and in many different ways
and that he could therefore learn something from
the old or from the contemporary representations; on
the opposite, he experiences the representation of the
woman like a blank field to which he has access for
the first time in his life. He loses himself so much that
his encounter with this new universe is transformed
into an adventure, without him knowing how far
it will take him. He ignores it at the beginning as
well as at the end – a moment when he should have
understood it! He doesn't know yet that what appears
in his hands will eventually represent a female
body. The experience of loss in a universe filled with
adventures is kept in such a way in his sculpture that
one doesn't feel the torso of a female body but rather
the fragment of a universe made dense – a fragment
of densified universe, yes, yet remaining open to
everything possible. So it is not a completed work,
like one is used to seeing. Listen: the older I get, the
more it seems impossible for me to complete a work.
A completed work is for me impossible to imagine! At
least it seems impossible as far as I'm concerned. One
leaves something that was the fruit of one day of work,
unable to carry on, then one starts something new,
compelled to start all over again.

Following a long conversation, here are my notes:
[*Giacometti:*] Since I was young, I've almost always imagined sculpture in colour. In our house in Maloja was a plaster bust of my father made by [Niederhausen-]Rodo. I couldn't stand the whiteness of the bust. It bore so little resemblance to my father! One day, my father being absent from the house for a brief moment, I decided to colour in the bust. I took my palette and my brush and set to work: I painted the eyes blue, the hair, moustache and beard red, the skin pink. I was very pleased with the result! I really thought it was only from that moment that the bust was completed and really represented a portrait of my father. I was convinced I was the person who had furnished the essential work.

He laughed, then his laugh turned into a smile that remained on his face for quite a while.

    — And what was your father's comment?

    — He was slightly taken aback. He might have thought I lacked respect for Rodo's work, but he didn't reproach me for it.

    Ah, he was very kind.

Then, after some thought:

    — Obviously, it's not what I mean to say when I say I see a sculpture in colour in front of my eyes. I don't see it coloured in a realist fashion, rather in greys, in a gradation of various hues of grey…

Gotthard Jedlicka, 'Alberto Giacometti, Fragmente aus Tagebüchern' (Fragments d'un journal), *Neue Zurcher Zeitung*, 5 April 1964, p. 4. Original translation from the German by Christiana Haack. Giacometti's words in bold are in French in the original text.

<u>I certainly practise painting…</u>

I certainly practise painting and sculpture and have
done since the very beginning, from the first time
I drew or painted, to bite into reality, to defend myself,
to feed myself, to grow; grow to defend myself better,
to attack better, to grip, to move forward as much as
possible on all levels, in all directions, to defend myself
against hunger, against cold, against death, to be the
freest possible; the freest possible to try–with the
means that are my very own today–to see better, to
comprehend better what is around me, to understand
better in order to be the freest, the biggest possible,
to spend, to exert myself as much as possible in what
I do, to live the adventure of my life, to discover new
worlds, to wage my own war, for the pleasure? for the
joy? of war, for the pleasure of winning and losing.

A reply to Pierre Voldboudt's enquiry 'To each person his reality'
in *XXe siècle*, no. 9, June 1957

<u>Grey,
brown,
black…</u>

Grey, brown, black, leaves, sands, vases; the big yellow
flowers are looking at me. I see myself amongst the
paintings, looking at them in turn, going from the
vase to the beach, the wheat, the shiny bicycle, the
damp meadow behind the two tree trunks on the
side of the road. I can feel the asphalt, the dust, the
expanse of the meadow and the forest, I am on the
road walking with that bicycle looking abandoned in
the landscape and then the bench under the trees in
the cool shade. I see the whole garden, I am in the
garden, I can hear footsteps on the gravel, the voice
of other people who are there with me, coming and
going, and, in the distance, there's that bench in the
cool shade, enticing me.

I look at the flowers. There are real flowers next
to the painting, they look alike. The window and
the objects, I go from the paintings to the objects;
together they create the room in which I am, which
I leave and which I enter again following the painting
I'm looking at and now, as I'm writing, I look at the
flowers that are there next to me on the table. They
have the same dimensions as Braque's flowers, the
same green too. I am not in my home, in my home
there's dust and darkness, it resembles less Braque's
paintings – and yet. Here, yes, and the landscape
surrounding me. Never have I been so struck by the
vast abundance of that marvellous big landscape.
Today I tried to paint it, I still have the bright
horizontal sky in front of my eyes and that density.
I think about what Braque said of the life-size
landscapes while looking at the Varengeville paintings,

life-size, like the Corot, which made me feel really happy. I knew then that he was right, tonight, I'm even more sure, and I also know that those flowers are life-size.

But how to describe his paintings? How to say the sensation stirred in me by the vertical barely out of alignment, of the vase and the flowers that rises on the grey background? That vertical of a slightly unstable balance is not traced; it emanates from the complexity of the forms and the colours that evoke the object. That vertical transformed into a line traced on a grey background (which, by the way, is impossible) would leave me rather indifferent. All the complexity of Cezanne's *Man with Crossed Arms* is essential for one to be gripped by one single stroke. The more a painting wants to give a representation of reality, the more I'm touched by the elements that, at first sight, don't seem to be the signs of the objects themselves, but are perhaps precisely those elements that end up recreating the vision of the object.

When I look at a leaf from the bouquet that is there, on the table, in front of me, by what am I seduced? Is it by the shape of the leaf or by its green colour, or by that same green standing out on the dark background? Is it by its situation in the bouquet as a whole or by the distance from table to leaf and from leaf to ceiling? Or by the drawing of its groves or by the white flower that comes forward in front of that same leaf, or rather by something else that I cannot articulate, that I cannot name, by that unknown that Braque evokes

for me in his very last paintings and that makes them
especially appealing to me.
They appeal to me because they are truly a good
likeness, that marvellous likeness that is shared by
all the painters I like, a likeness that is as multiple
as those paintings and that enables an object to
exist, infinite on a canvas. That painting enables me
to look slightly differently at the objects that in turn,
shed some light on the painting. Those paintings
of whatever period are for me contemporary and all
are like an open question, but at the same time the
flowers and leaves are there in front of me as if nobody
had ever seen them. But why, of all of Braque's latest
paintings, is it the yellow-ochre vase that remained
the most vivid in my memory? Perhaps because by
hanging there, by giving such a weight to one single
part of the surface of the simplest and, in a way, the
most significant of objects, he highlights at the same
time everything he doesn't paint, he enhances the
dullest and worthless things, and magnifies all those
things that exceed them as far as the one who looks
at them.

Braque, trying to preserve those perishable flowers,
Braque, hopeless it seems facing those things he
questions, trying to fix on a canvas for a little longer,
for the longest time possible, a fragment of all those
things and himself and the others.
Trying to save something from the immense
cavernous darkness that surrounds them, that eats
at them from all sides, but no! The paintings are the
most fragile, we are the most fragile, not the flowers.

The flowers impassively continue to grow and their darkness is not ours.
I go to the window, I look outside in the night, the dark mountain, the sky sparkling with so many stars and the sound of water. Yes, men continue too like flowers, never exactly the same, but they paint and that changes everything.

*

But why, why do flowers seem marvellous to us?

Stampa. May 1952.

Derrière le miroir, no. 48-49, June-July 1952, accompanying the exhibition "Georges Braque" at the Galerie Maeght, Paris, n.p.

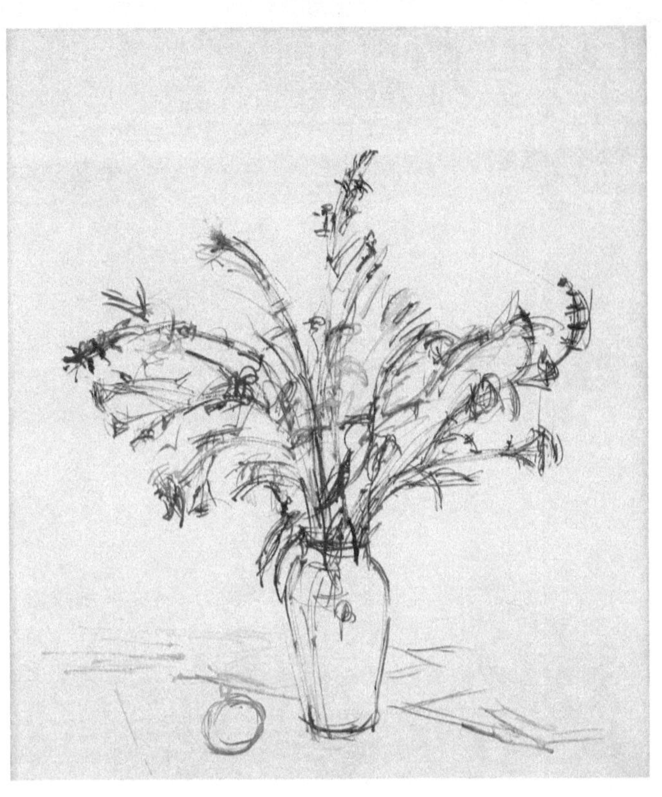

Bouquet and Apple, c. 1961
Oil on canvas
46.5 x 55 cm
Fondation Giacometti

<u>Braque has just died</u>

Georges Braque has just died. This news doesn't strike any chord in me at this moment. Georges Braque remains for this moment as alive as he was in the past, more alive than ever perhaps, somewhere in his house, in his studio, here in Paris, or at the seaside, coming and going, from one painting to the next, smoking his cigarette. I can see myself at his place, listening to him, talking, a cup of coffee in front of us on the little table as it has been the case countless times since 1930. But at the same time, I think with nostalgia of the distant past of Montmartre that I didn't experience. I think about the young men who were Braque, Picasso and their friends, I see them in their daily life and their so-called 'cubist' paintings are for me before all else, the documents, the reflections even of that daily life; for them they made concrete the vast and thrilling beginning of a new future and the immediate freshness of all things. Then this future became for each of them a complex and solitary path.
Tonight, the whole oeuvre of Georges Braque becomes again contemporary for me; straight out of time, it is situated in space. From that whole oeuvre I view with the most interest, curiosity and emotion, the small landscapes, the still lifes, the modest bouquets of the last, the very last years. I look at that almost unassertive painting, intangible, this naked painting, of a completely different boldness, a much greater boldness than that of the distant past; a painting that is for me at the very edge of art today with all its conflicts.

Les Lettres françaises, no. 993, 5-11 September 1963, p. 1 and 10

Portrait of an artist (VIII)
Giacometti
In conversation with
Alain Jouffroy

One feels there is no one behind that grey door with dusty windows; an old piece of fabric prevents us seeing through the window of that small studio. We push open the door. Between tall white sculptures, unfinished or half-destroyed, under an electric lamp that harshly lights up the wall with pink and yellow faded colours, near a small couch covered in newspapers, books and a few canvases leaning against the wall, here's Giacometti, quietly seated on a high stool, in the process of sculpting a figure in clay. He knows the object of my visit, and immediately tries to postpone it.

— It's not the best time. It has never been a worse time than today. You've come at the wrong time. Perhaps in a week or so it will be perfect… I've been working on those figures for months. I'm going to work on them throughout the winter. But if I end up having four or five sculptures in six months or nothing at all, it's exactly the same to me. That it fails or that it succeeds, it's the same thing: each time I win.

He sees me writing this last sentence:

— Oh no, don't write that!

— *Why?*

— Because once it's written, it takes on a different meaning. When one speaks, the sentence that comes before and the one that comes after make it ambiguous. That it goes very well or very badly, it's the same thing. Or rather: it only goes very well because it goes very badly.

*He leaves for a moment. I take off my coat: it's warm.
I feel I'm about to witness a fight: that of Giacometti
with himself. I recognise on the couch a portrait of his
wife Annette and still lifes of small bottles: these seem to
have been placed on the work table a hundred of years ago,
covered as they are with dust.
He comes back and continues:*

— No, it's not that I doubt…

*No, I know, Giacometti doesn't 'doubt'. He knows what
he's doing, or rather he knows exactly the difficulties of
what he undertakes, he doesn't conceal them from himself.
He faces up to them every day: he doesn't undo today what
he did the previous day, as it would be too easy to say that,
he sees the contradictions inherent in the nature of things.
Its contradictions are not those he sees, permanent, in
reality itself: and it's those he wants to communicate.
He tells me how it all began: how he only stayed at
Geneva's Fine Art school three days because his teacher
tried to force him to put 'volumes' in the head he had
made him do from life; that his sculpture, thin as a leaf,
only got thicker little by little; how he had an argument
with his teacher, at the Ecole des Arts et Métiers in the
same town, because the latter wanted Giacometti to put
a 'dark background' behind his nude, while he didn't see
'any more shade in the background than on the face of the
model'. He talks about his father, Giovanni Giacometti,
a Swiss Impressionist painter who, in 1921, took him to
visit Venice, where the young Alberto didn't want to miss
one single painting by Tintoretto; Florence, where he saw
for the first time an Egyptian sculpture that 'gave him the*

feeling of reality and made him land on his feet'; Assisi, where he discovered Cimabue, who totally eclipsed in his eyes the Renaissance painters; and finally Rome, where he stayed for eight months and attended an evening class; it was in Rome that he undertook the making of two busts he never completed and finally destroyed the moment he left.

— Those two busts I failed to make successfully in Rome thirty-five years ago are definitely the busts I'm trying to make today.

The following year, in 1922, his father sent him to Paris where Bourdelle was teaching at the Grande Chaumière. He worked there for four years.

— Since the very beginning, strangely, the idea of a sculpture not painted, seemed absurd to me. I used to have the model come to my studio and I painted the plaster from life. I wanted to show it to Bourdelle: but when I brought it to the studio, there was such a commotion among the other students that I gave up on the idea.

— *But you started making abstract sculptures at that time, no?*

— I exhibited one at the Salon des Tuileries in 1925. Bourdelle said: 'You can do that at home, but don't show it.'

— *Then you took part in Surrealism...*

— Yes, and it was the statue Breton liked best,
The Invisible Object, that disrupted everything in my
life again. I was satisfied with the hands and the head
of that sculpture because they corresponded exactly
with my idea. But I was not happy at all with the legs,
the torso and the breasts. They seemed too academic,
too conventional. And that gave me the desire to work
again from life.

*We are now at the heart of the problem Giacometi has been
trying to solve since then:*

— One only sees reality through screens. People
only see the world through the works of academic
painting, or Impressionist painting. In the same way
in sculpture, everyone thinks he knows what a head
is, but everyone sees a Greco-Roman bust in place
of the head. Today, any country folk see the shadows
as violet; the posters in the station have made him
accept that without him realising. For me now, reality
no longer resembles Impressionist painting at all.
I thought it was Cezanne and the Impressionists
who came the closest to reality (when I was 16,
I was making divisionist paintings). Now, between
what I see in the street and Impressionist painting,
there's a chasm.

*— What happened when you went back to work
from life?*

— To my great surprise, I realised that what
I was doing had nothing to do with the model I saw.

To make the work easier, I placed the model further
away, and the bust was getting gradually smaller.
I realised I didn't see reality. But trying to see it as it is
seemed to me more exciting than all the compositions
I could make. What is a head, nobody in the world
can explain that to me. I see you, I hear you at the
same time, it's all very complex. It's more complex
than we can express. Your head is something else than
what I believe I see and what I imagine. If I tried to
paint it for a thousand years, every day I would see it
slightly different, it would be a never-ending task.

*— So you are trying to have a more 'original' vision
of things than the vision given by academic painters,
by the Impressionists…*

— What is strange is that one believes
photography gives a more faithful image of the world
than painting. Even an abstract painter shows you the
photograph of his children. For me, the photograph
of a street is slightly more remote from the street
than a Byzantine painting of the street would be.
I noticed that in 1946, when I went to see a film at
the Actualités Montparnasse. Suddenly (that came
from the drawings I was making at the time), the
only thing I saw were black spots moving on a white
surface. I was so struck that I no longer saw the image
those spots represented. When I left the cinema, I was
taken aback: it was as if I was seeing the boulevard
Montparnasse for the first time. It no longer had
anything in common with the image on the screen.

He shows me then Annette's portrait, still far from being finished.

— It seems to me totally impossible to paint a head in that dimension. It seems to me I don't have the means to do that. It's a shame.

And Giacometti says he will work on that painting for the whole winter.

'Portrait d'un artiste (VIII) Giacometti' in *Arts*,
no. 545, 7-13 December 1955

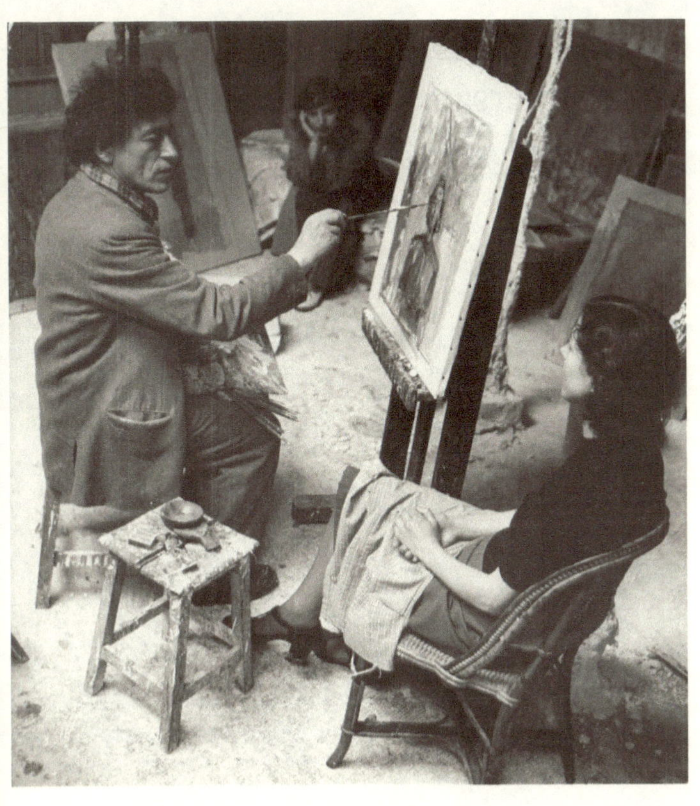

Alberto Giacometti painting the portrait of Annette in the studio, 1951
Photo: Ernst Scheidegger
Fondation Giacometti Archives

The painter's monologue
In conversation with Georges Charbonnier

Alberto Giacometti, when I started this series of programmes entitled 'The Painter's Monologue', I didn't have a very clear preconceived idea. In the series, there are abstract painters, there are figurative painters, there are so-called 'realist' painters, well, painters from different tendencies. At the beginning, I didn't plan to move in a very precise direction and, above all, I didn't want to stir a quarrel between abstraction and non-abstraction, figuration and non-figuration. These are words painters don't like and I think they encompass very solid things. Nevertheless, it is the idea of reality around which the whole series of broadcasts is organised. So you, for example, do you consider yourself a realist painter?

— If one says 'realist painter', surely, immediately, someone imagines a certain kind of realism, no?

— Of course…

— And usually, one imagines to be realist something that, precisely, is very little realist, I mean a conventional realism, which is just academism.

— That's to say things that one recognises easily.

— One thinks about a painting that represents external reality in the most uninspired manner, doesn't it?

— Absolutely!

— Most people whom you ask what is the realist representation of a woman will answer Bouguereau rather than Cezanne. That's for sure.

— *That's for sure.*

— I have friends who pretended to like, let's say, Picasso, because he doesn't work on likeness. And they said however that they see reality as Bouguereau. And they absolutely wanted to make me say that it's the same thing for me. If that was true, I would prefer Bouguereau to Picasso or Cezanne, since what interests me, after all, in all paintings, is the likeness, what, for me, is the likeness: what makes me discover a little the outside world that I see…

— *What you call 'likeness' is it not what the spectators you're talking about, call 'likeness'?*

— No, not at all. To begin with, yes; to begin with, it's probably the same thing…

— *There's the same medium, but there's not the same way of seeing.*

— There's the same medium. But the difference is probably very complex. Someone who doesn't know painting at all, or knows a certain painting, let's say, who stops at the painting of 1900, he knows photographs, he sees a reproduction of a woman by Bouguereau, it's immediately a woman… He will recognise it as such. Even more, if she's

pretty, the likeness and desire intervene to find in
the painting almost the ideal of reality. Probably…
with lots of people.

*— It's certain that realism, for the common spectator,
is tainted with idealism.*

— One only has to go to the Louvre, on a winter
Sunday, when it's crowded. Where are the most people
gathered? In front of *The Coronation of Napoleon*. And
why do people look at that painting? First because
they imagine they are witnessing the scene, taking part.
And they become, a little bit, a small 'Napoleon' at the
same time. It becomes, to some extent, the equivalent
of reading a novel, in which they identify a little bit
with the hero or the heroine, doesn't it? They would
rather look at the *Coronation* than a painting
by Chardin.

*— That spectator who demands realism is the
same one who wants boxing matches and who admires*
The Coronation of Napoleon.

— Yes, but it's also the same one who spends his
holidays in Brittany, likes the sea, the sun and walking,
and who buys, on the boulevard Raspail, a painting of
Brittany. Obviously he buys the painting that prolongs
or fixes the sensations he likes the best in life. He
doesn't look at it like a professional, or like people who
work in the arts, and who think it's a bad painting…
Those, if they think the painting is bad, despise it
because an evolution has taken place especially since

Impressionism where one began to become involved
with the painting for the painting, where the painting
was created that can claim it represents outside reality
less and less….
For anyone pretending to be knowledgeable and who's
really involved in the arts, it would feel below him
to look at a landscape of Brittany on the boulevard
Raspail, or a naked woman with cherries in her hair on
the walls of a restaurant. There are paintings, I mean,
at La Palette, I think precisely of certain paintings, in
restaurants, paintings of the type I look at when I'm
having dinner… and I look at them with the same
curiosity as at any masterpiece.
But there's a divide that happens in the public,
between the public who continue to consider in the
painting the subject solely, as far as forgetting [the
painter] – they don't even bother to seek who made it,
it's the subject that takes precedence – and the public
who looks, in the painting, for the expression of the
painter himself, don't you agree?
It is that public who no longer goes to see the
Coronation or then those who look at it do so in a
totally different way. They look at it because it's by
David. They look at it because it's against… It's a new
conception of painting, of vision.

— *They look at it for the organisation of the painting.*

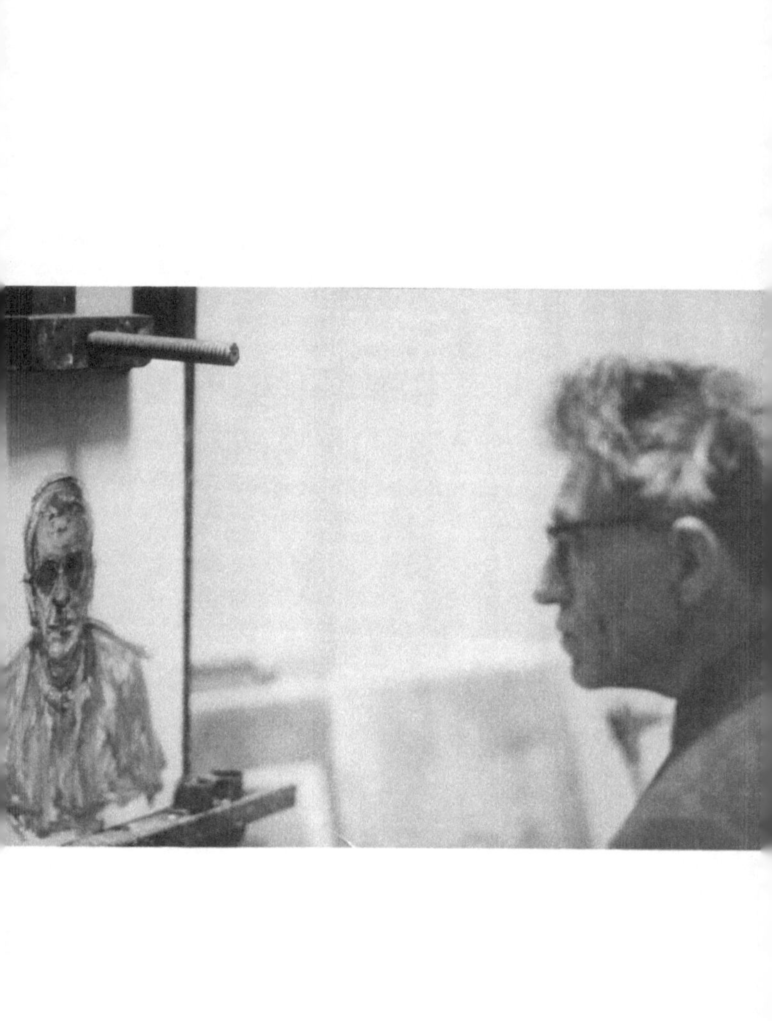

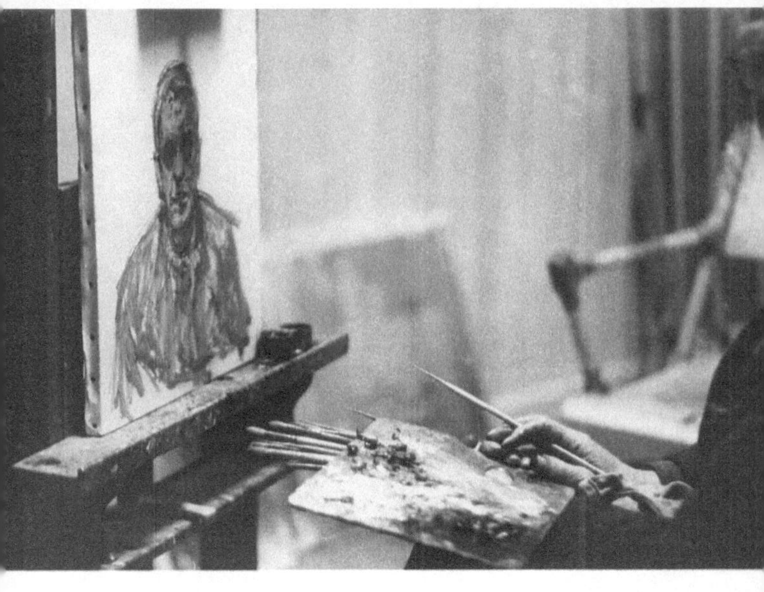

Alberto Giacometti in his studio in Stampa,
painting the portrait of Giorgio Soavi, 1963
Photo: Giorgio Soavi
Fondation Giacometti Archives

<u>I go against the flow</u>
In conversation with
Marie-Thérèse Maugis

After Michel Butor and Jean-Marie Le Clézio, Christian Zervos, Serge Poliakoff and Pierre Soulages, here's Alberto Giacometti at the time when the room that is devoted to him at the Fondation Maeght perhaps gives to the public, finally, the real measure of his artistic talent.

— Giacometti, do you think that what really represents an era is its art?

— Of course. What's left of prehistory but works of art? What's left of Egypt but works of art? As soon as people possess the means to write, the writing also remains… If one talks about Greece, there's philosophy, poetry, art… Art is always the expression of its era.

— But isn't the knowledge one has of art particularly developed today?

— Of course, that also. Through photographs and travels, we are familiar with art from its very beginning. The Impressionists, Cezanne, were familiar with the art that started with the Renaissance. For them, the rest was archaeology. For the Venetians, for the Flemish, Byzantine art was barely art at all. Today, we have a different vision: we are familiar with Negro art, Oceanic art, prehistoric art, etc. We know works of art from all civilisations have remained. We also can make the difference between a Greek sculpture and a Greek chariot… If a sculpture of any civilisation disappears for a time, it can reappear and influence contemporary art. That's what happened

with archaic art twenty years ago. It's not the same
process for objects: the modern car abolished the
chariot drawn by a horse. But a work of art is never
surpassed. In this field, one cannot speak of progress.
To say which art today is the expression of our time
is quite difficult. There are painters who reproduce
the Moulin Rouge or St Mark's Square, others who
paint landscapes from Brittany or bouquets of roses.
There are abstract painters, constructivists, tachists,
sub-Impressionists, post-Impressionists, it all seems
on opposite sides, but to tell the truth, all are the
expression of our time…

*— Do you think the multiplication of so-called
artistic expressions generates a greater interest for those
activities?*

— Today, it's not going very well. The Arts
today are becoming more and more abstract. On
top of that, there's pop art. There are also all those
who exhibit at La Palette, those one calls easy and
who, again, are appreciated by a certain retrograde
bourgeoisie. There's official art too, which is avant-
garde art. But since the cubists, only a very small
portion of civilisation is interested in art. The rest are
interested in postcards. For the vast majority of people,
art is well and truly television, cinema, a doll, posters,
promotional items, everything that, specifically, is not
considered art. I was one of the jury in the Biennale
des Jeunes and I don't know if you remember an
Italian artist who had made an all-red painting. Two
workmen who were standing around cutting some

planks were stupefied. It was a laugh for them to see serious people considering that red painting and judging it. When Schöeffer makes luminous objects that revolve, it's outmoded, a juke-box gives as much and more, it's luminous, it's amusing, it moves. It is, I believe, what explains the interest in pop art. Pop art is more interesting for the public than spots on a canvas. It shows posters and photographs to advantage. But do you think Rauschenberg can carry on sticking Kennedy on a canvas? Did you notice pop art is suddenly catching up with Soviet socialist realism? Apart from the subject, there's only one step between them. You'll see the Russians evolve too… Two years ago, the movement already started with poetry. You'll see them do photomontages very soon…

— Do you think that effervescence of art and para-art activities is a speciality of our time?

— Art has always moved with great speed. In Egyptian sculpture, which seemed static for three or four millennia, it is possible to distinguish eras and, in spite of the apparent rigidity of the forms, one notices an extraordinary renewal every 50 years or so. On the opposite, today one pretends there's an enormous chasm between the discredited paintings of La Palette, and the cubists and modern art. They are all much closer to one another than one thinks… For example, the vision of colours remains Impressionist. The painters have not moved one step from there. They all give an enormous supremacy to colour and therefore use colours… I rigorously look with the

same interest at the most pompous painting hanging
on a restaurant's walls as at a painting by those we call
today's great painters!

— Do you think they belong to the same art sphere?

— Obviously we have to limit the spheres…
A vase, as beautiful as it is, is not a sculpture, it's an
object. It's another domain. This vase only refers to
itself. But when one produces a painting that only
represents itself, sooner or later it disappears. When
Duchamp exhibited a chair, for him art was finished…
And all those who make ceramics as if they had
succeeded in their paintings, they don't carry on
with their work, they simply go from one domain to
another. It's for that reason a so-called painting by
Rauschenberg is closer to what is a painting than what
an abstract can do. He does something clever really, by
sticking a Velasquez or a Titian he refers to something
else than himself. Red tiles, even well painted, are still
only red tiles. Writing itself only has meaning for you
as it says something other than signs. In that sense,
Letterism can only have a short life. One can listen
to a couple of lettrist poems, three are already one
too many…

*— Yes, but doesn't the progress in techniques and
the greater knowledge one has of things, upon which you
were reflecting earlier, inevitably lead to an evolution in
painting, as in writing?*

— Of course… It's not by chance that with
the discovery of photography, artists stopped making
portraits. Before, one could only represent someone
by making a painting. And if we can mechanically
give a vision of the outside world, we do without
the use of the hand. It's so obvious that if a painter,
seeing a man running, started to paint him, he would
look old-fashioned… as would the person who, after
the discovery of the printing process, would have
continued writing books by hand… But what's
important is that the Impressionists, and the
painters who came after, cubists included, carried
on representing something…

— *The abstracts, not representing anything, don't
express anything, then?*

— A painter cannot not represent something.
It's absolutely inevitable. It's a necessity. It's also
obvious that modern art, through the posters or
the architectures of bars and cafés, enters the public
domain. There's no doubt about it, as there's no
doubt either that all art influences well and truly
the physiognomy of an epoch. Whether it's good
or mediocre…

— *But you Giacometti, who paint and sculpt faces,
living beings whose image haunts you, do you have the
feeling you're representing your time?*

— For me, the problem is different. I was very
young when I began to make drawings and sculptures

because my father was a painter. I will never know if
I would have become what I am, if I would have made
what I make if my father hadn't been a painter. We
go back to the problem of the milieu, the class. But I
never wished to make painting a profession. Even in
my youth, art was certainly the representation of the
outside world, or of something, in any case. There are
two veins in art. Either you try to render the outside
world as you see it, or you tell stories… And that from
the very beginning. And those two veins are equally
relevant. In Rembrandt, a portrait which is an image
that's the most faithful, the most lifelike, is as relevant
as the illustrations for the Old Testament. Rousseau,
who painted tropical forests with monkeys, is as
relevant as Matisse who was making the portrait of
his daughter. Those two movements are still relevant.
Those whose research is solely one-sided are rare.
As for Chardin, with his still lifes, he only pursues
the closest representation of reality that is possible.
Delacroix or Géricault have already expanded their
art. One can paint *The Raft of the Medusa* or make a
portrait of a mad woman. Both paths continue with
Picasso who can paint the portrait of a specific person
or represent scenes that come close to mythology.
I'll repeat, one path is as relevant as the other. The
Impressionists, in general, remain solely focussed on
a vision of the outside world.

— *But you, in which movement do you situate
yourself?*

— Until 1925, despite my interest for modern

art, what interested me was the vision of the outside
world, strictly, as closely as possible. In 1925, I
realised it was impossible for me to reproduce a head.
Influenced by modern art, I evolved. I was successively
exotic, surrealist, abstract… In 1935, having forgotten
everything, I felt again the need to make studies from
life; I went back to experimental work. My problem is
to comprehend why it is impossible for me to do what
I want to do. I try every night to make a head and
I can't do it. Every night I try to perceive what I see
and why I can't manage to represent it.
Once again, in a certain society, I wouldn't be
able to spend my time doing that. I don't work to
communicate something to other people, but to
discover if I could one day make a sculpture or a
painting. What I do is probably obsolete before I even
do it. I'm not sure there's a future in sculpture made
that way. But if I represent a model like I do, even
though I am wide of the mark, and given that I have
the possibility to do it, it's because I'm curious to
know what I see in a head. I am compelled to make
the sculpture or the painting to comprehend what
I see. In that respect I don't think I am the expression
of our epoch. I cannot even say…

*— Those faces that you continually copy are not
anonymous. They can only give you an awareness of today's
world through what they are…*

— Undoubtedly, but one face is worth any
other face.

Those I paint are chosen from chance encounters. Any face is a good face. And I, immobile in front of an immobile face, trying to apprehend what it is I see: that could happen in any epoch, couldn't it! Between your head in front of that wall and that of a prehistoric man, there's probably no difference at all. The relation between what characterises one epoch and another is rather precarious. Personally I go completely against the flow. I am the only one who tries only to copy. And what I copy is that tiny residue I remain aware of through looking. Copying is the daftest thing in the world, copying a glass for example, but there's nothing more difficult. In reality it's impossible, Cezanne said more or less, to copy from life is impossible, one can only interpret it. That didn't stop him copying right up to his death… As I know I will never succeed in copying a head as I see it, it seems like an aberration to insist doing it, and it's probably an aberration. It's even a total absurdity, what I'm trying to do. So it's impossible for me to imagine what a finished painting would be like and it is the reason I go against the flow compared to the other painters in modern art who always complete all their paintings, and do so in one day even. I know I can work all my life on one painting without ever finishing it. And, supposing I live for 300 or 400 years, I still wouldn't achieve it, ever.

— I am obviously conditioned by my past, my time. It is commonplace to say so. A conventional painter or an extremely modern painter are conditioned by their epoch. On top of that, everything one does, one does through necessity, and that red dot on a blank canvas can only be painted that day, at that place, in those circumstances. It's quite simple, really. Everything that is made, everything that is created is of some interest. That's the reason why I would like, when one attacks Rauschenberg, to be told why he is not worthy of the human species! To be told why what he does is rubbish, without defending the stable values that have a value in the bank. I'm interested in pop art, actually. And the abstracts, the extreme edge of modern art, must be bothered by that, right? The one who puts three colours when the other exhibits margarine in bulk, it's funny, no?

— I think however that the dispute around pop art today is rather superficial, more from the point of view of fashion, really.

— Yes, but it goes far. What is funny is that Pop art is not art! It's not that which will stop me coming closer to my model's ear. What can be said about Rauschenberg though, is that he's clever when he sticks a photo of Kennedy, a falcon, reminiscent of Egypt, a Venus by Titian or by Rubens. All we can say is that it resembles a deck of cards: whatever he puts in, it works. The means are the same as those of Dada, but the purpose is not the same. I don't see why he wouldn't make use of the means we used thirty

years ago! Apart from that I want to say, and I am
almost the only person saying it, and I was surprised
by the reviews in Les Lettres françaises, that the
pavilion I liked best at the Venice Biennale in 1962,
was that of the USSR. At least they tried, as best they
could, to represent something… Today, when each
person wants to represent their individuality, I give
no importance to mine. We have never seen, though,
so many similar paintings in the whole world, and of
such good taste… At least the Russian paintings were
not very successful… I particularly remember one
that represented two lorries on a bridge: there was the
beginning of a certain vision.
Have you ever seen perfect paintings? Personally I
have never seen one. It's one of the characteristics of
art, actually. The helix of a plane, in order to function,
must be perfect, a wineglass, to be usable, mustn't be
chipped. On the opposite, a work of art is only ever a
partial vision of the outside world, always precarious
too. In painting, in sculpture as in poetry, there
cannot be perfection. That's what gives them interest,
virulence or violence. I already told you that, the
bad paintings of an artist interest me as much as the
good ones. For me, there's no difference. Anyway, one
exaggerates the importance one gives to Art with a big
'A'. The majority of people don't give a toss.

— Do you believe that was always the case?

— Perhaps less in the Middle Ages, when art
was at the service of the organisation of the state.
For the majority of people in a small town, their

cathedral counted a lot, for sure, because they didn't
have anything else to get their teeth into. Given the
people's religious beliefs, if someone said he was not
interested in God, he was burnt alive. So at that time
art was a necessity.

*— Do you think that there are too many possible
distractions, too many leisure activities today?*

— Yes, surely, art is no longer a necessity.
Paintings go directly from the studio to the museum.
It's quite precarious as a journey, no? And the little
white horse that's used to advertise the White Horse
whisky is more necessary than the masterpieces
of great artists. I personally don't consider myself
more useful to society than the DIY enthusiast who
enjoys tinkering with bits and pieces. I don't give
such importance to my painting. Everything interests
me, but one can only do something well when one
limits oneself to the extreme. That what I do is useful
or not is the least of my worries. It's there too that
my position opposed that of today's painters who
consider they have a role to play in society; I am also
against social benefits for artists: one only does art at
one's own perils and I'm also aware that society can
perfectly do without what I do.

Les Lettres françaises, no. 1041, 6-19 August 1964, p. 1 and 14

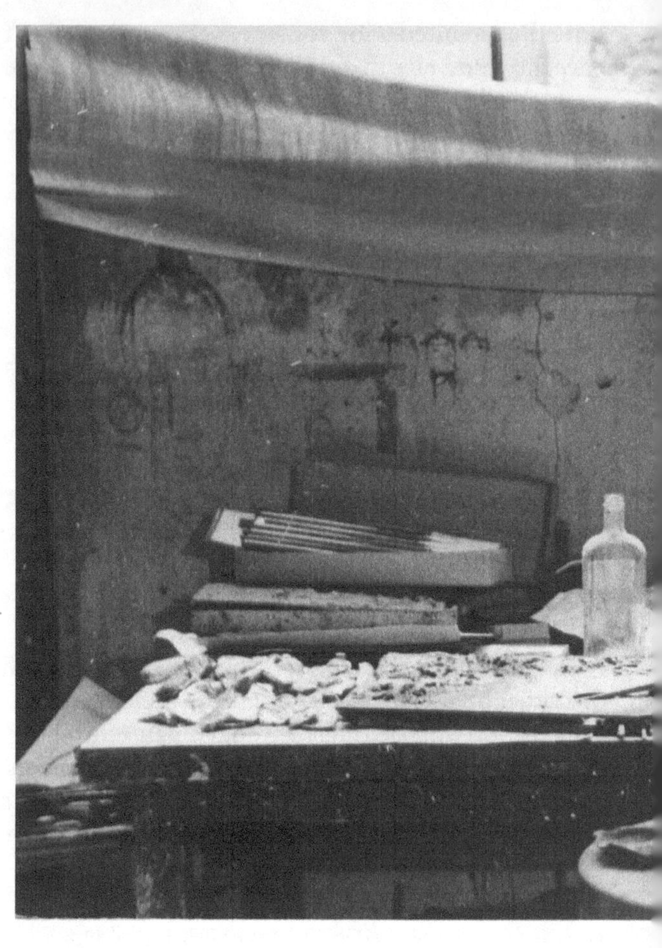

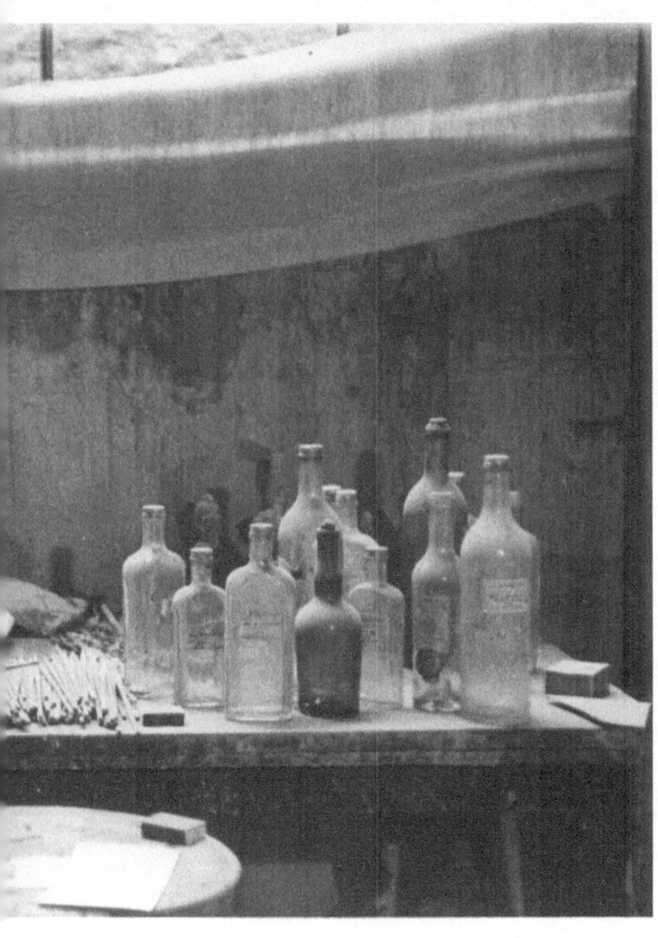

Table underneath the window in Giacometti's studio, c. 1957-1958
Unknown photographer
Fondation Giacometti Archives

<u>paintings</u>
heads
half-figures
figures
dressed nudes
still lifes – interiors
landscapes
(compositions)
all that.

<u>drawings</u>
<u>all and nudes.</u>

penknife.
As quickly as possible go back to all that, as quickly as
possible painting too, buy canvases.

1960

Translated from French by Paul Buck and Catherine Petit.

Cover: Alberto Giacometti painting the Hippolyte-Maindron street,
summer 1952
Photo Roger Montandon
Fondation Giacometti Archives

ISBN : 979 1 0370 1681 2